R̶e̶d̶l̶a̶n̶d̶s̶

£ 5-00

GW01466584

By the same author

NOVELS
The Circle
The Amberstone Exit
The Glass Alembic
Children of the Rose
The Ecstasy of Dr Miriam Garner
The Shadow Master
The Survivors
The Border

SHORT STORIES
The Silent Areas

BIOGRAPHY
Bessie Smith
A Captive Lion: the Life of Marina Tsvetayeva

POEMS
In a Green Eye
The Celebrants
The Magic Apple Tree
Some Unease and Angels
Translations
Three Russian Poets
The Selected Poems of Marina Tsvetayeva

Badlands

Elaine Feinstein

Hutchinson

London Melbourne Auckland Johannesburg

Copyright © Elaine Feinstein 1986

First published in Great Britain in 1986 by Century Hutchinson Ltd
Brookmount House, 62–65 Chandos Place, Covent Garden, London
WC2N 4NW

Century Hutchinson Publishing Group (Australia) Pty Ltd
16–22 Church Street, Hawthorn, Melbourne, Victoria 3122

Century Hutchinson (NZ) Ltd
32–34 View Road, PO Box 40-086, Glenfield, Auckland 10

Century Hutchinson Group (SA) Pty Ltd
PO Box 337, Bergvlei 2012, South Africa

Set in 11/12pt Bembo by
Rowland Phototypesetting Ltd
Bury St Edmunds, Suffolk

Some of these poems have appeared in the *New Statesman*, *Poetry Nation Review*, and *Slipping Past*; and three of the lyrics from 'Dido and Aeneas' appeared in *The Border*. 'Songs for Eurydice' appeared in Next Editions.

Printed and bound in Great Britain by
The Guernsey Press Co. Ltd
Guernsey, Channel Islands

ISBN 0 09 165740 7

For Adam

Contents

A Letter from La Jolla

On a balcony in California
being surprised by February
which is the sweet season here, when
blue-scaled grunion dance
on their tails, at high tide
on La Jolla sands, to matc there
and are caught in pails and eaten,

I write across distance and so much time
to ask, my one-time love, what happened to you?
Since my last letter which I meant to be
cruel as my own hurt could barb it, now
under yellow skies, pale sun, I sit
sucking fresh limes and thinking over
my childish spite, and how much life I've wasted.

I'm jealous of the sensible girl
you must have married long since.
Well, I've been happy, too.
Sometimes. You always knew
the shape I'd choose would never
be single or sober, and you did not need
what you once most admired.

Unswerving as you were, I guess
you must be prosperous, your children neat,

I

less beautifully unruly than my own
perhaps less talented, less generous;
and you won't know my work or my new name,
nor ever read my books.
Our worlds don't meet.

And yet I doubt if you have altogether
forgotten the unsuitable dark girl
you held all weekend in your parents' flat,
talking and talking, so this letter
comes to you this morning almost in play:
our thoughts once moved so easily together
like dolphins offshore to the land mass of the day.

The Water Magician of San Diego

For Joel

A blue pool wobbles in the sun.
Above me, like ocean weeds,
the strands of palm leaves flicker;
sticky ferns unroll their fronds;
the red helicopters hum,
like summer birds overhead;
and a local voice inquires:
How are you doing today.
What can I possibly say?

I'm trying to recover, but
I haven't quite learnt the smile.
And it may take quite a while
to look out over this ocean
that covers most of the planet
and not feel (mainly) alone.
My neighbour in the deckchair
is a Californian male.
And he senses a foreign spirit.

My books and scribble betray it.
So far he's not alarmed.
His handsome face is dimpled.
His hair cut short as fur;

and he has no fear of failure.
Don't wish him any harm,
but I'd like to see him waver.
– Hatfield, I murmur, Hatfield.
– Don't think I follow that.

– Don't you remember him?
He doesn't, and he finds my words
both dubious and grim.
– These, I say, are the Badlands,
won back from the dry brush and buzzard
for the entrepreneur and the bandit
these old hills, (the gold hills) favour.
Nowadays the realtors
take breakfast at La Valencia.

He doesn't understand. But
my eyes are deep and burning.
My face is aquiline.
I bring a whiff of danger;
Something is out of hand.
Perhaps I've fallen into
need (or even worse) bad luck,
which are sinister contagions
nobody here laughs off.

– Shall I confess the facts?
I've lived for five years now
as love's hypochondriac, and
it's hard to break the habit.
Is that what you're picking up?

4

Do you guess I've carried here
some intractable history?
(I'm teasing, but his face betrays
he's sorry now he woke me.)

– Hatfield the rainmaker?
He asks uneasily.
– The same, I nod, folk hero.
A native of your city.
A farm near San Diego
housed his earliest chemistry.
I thought you'd know his name.
Once City Halls in every County
echoed to his fame.

You needed him for water
on which this coast depends.
This strip may look like Paradise
but garden life could end.
Nothing here is natural.
The ice-plant spreads magenta
but these trees aren't indigenous.
Your water's brought from Boulder
and sprinklers cool the citrus.

Which is why you need magicians
(He's looking rather pale).
You will remember Hamelin?
No. Europe is far away.
The burghers learnt a lesson there.
Magicians must be paid.

5

Comfort and complacency
bring in their own revenge –
– The whole thing's superstition!

– No doubt, I nod to this,
And yet his contracts were fulfilled.
The clouds formed as he promised,
the reservoirs were filled.
He was modest in his offer
to those areas parched for rain;
he set evaporating tanks about,
his only claim, within a month,
Nature would end the drought.

He came when men were waiting.
Made an educated bet.
The councillors who hired him
must have known as much, and yet
they paid their fifty dollars out
with unconcealed relief.
The snag in San Diego
was the absence of belief.

Newspapers counted down the days
and gloated as they passed.
For being taken in, they mocked
the Mayor and all his staff.
(The charlatan's forgiven here
but no one trusts a victim.)
Lawyers sent to Hatfield
made manoeuvres which he met

with sardonic understanding,
and at once planned his departure.
The careful and the sober
should treat with great respect
whoever lives upon his wits.
Con-men, poker-players, poets
put the solid world at risk
and then enjoy the dance;
what happened then was in excess
of meteorological variance.

Rain? More than sixteen inches.
Flooded freeways, and carried off bridges.
There were bungalows dragged off their moorings.
And houses perched up on the cliff edge.
There was furniture floating on drainage.
There were hailstones like hens' eggs, and flashes
that carved out a creek through the desert.
Then mass panic.
Evacuation.

Abandoning motor transport,
in rowboats, on surf boards and planks
the rich mostly got away early
but they couldn't call in at the banks.
My neighbour said with conviction:
They'd have lynched him!
But I shook my head: It seems
Hatfield's contracts continued.
And the law wasn't ever called in.

My neighbour can't lie in his deckchair.
Perhaps he should take a quick swim?
Or calm his nerves in the Jacuzzi.
I feel almost friendly to him.
– Three wives, I should guess, lie behind you.
You're rich and you're healthy, and free.
Don't be anxious
or look for an answer
to some threat you imagine in me.

If I ever succeed in escaping
from this future where I am a stranger
and find myself back home in Europe
with those I most love out of danger;
as I fly back on some scheduled airline
(putting all my old pennies together)
when my spirit revives, I may well be
peppery, bold and alert there.
But I won't interfere with the weather.

Home

Where is that I wonder?
Is it the book-packed house we plan to sell
with the pale green room above the river,
the shelves of icons, agate, Eilat stone
the Kathe Kollwitz and the Samuel Palmer?

Or my huge childhood house
oak-floored, the rugs of Autumn colours, slabs of coal
in an open hearth, high-windowed rooms,
outside, the sunken garden, lavender, herbs
and trees of Victoria plum.

Last night I dreamed of
my dead father, white-faced, papery-skinned
and frailer than he died. I asked him:
– Doesn't all this belong to us? He shook his head,
bewildered. I was disappointed,

but though I woke with salt on my lips then
and a hoarse throat, somewhere between
the ocean and the desert, in an immense
Mexico of the spirit, I remembered
with joy and love my other ties of blood.

Remembering Brecht

'The man who laughs has not yet heard the appalling news'

That April, even though the trees were grey
   with something more than winter, when
I heard your voice and felt the first tremor
   of recovery, my joy was most mistaken,

which is not to say that living clenched with terror
   offers any protection. Other surprises
wait upon tears. Whatever we devise
   things may get worse.

Don't cry.   They often do.

Regret

Do not look backward, children.
A sticky burning sea still lies below.
The harsh air stings like sand

and here among these salty pillars
the unforgiving stand. Take
the mountain ledge, even though

it crumbles into dust. Walk or crawl,
you must let the rocks cut into your feet without pity.
And forget the smoking city. God punishes regret.

England

Forgotten, shabby and long time abandoned
    in stubbled fur, with broken
teeth like toggles, the old gods are leaving.
    They will no longer crack the
tarmac of the language, open generous
    rivers, heal our scoured thoughts.
They will only blink, and move on, and
    tomorrow no one will remember their songs

unless they rise in warning, as when
    sudden planes speed overhead
crossing the sky with harsh accelerating
    screams. You may shiver then
to hear the music of the gods leaving.
    This generation
is waiting for the boy Octavius.
    They don't like losers.
And the gods are leaving us.

Rose

Your pantry stocked with sweet cooked fish,
   pink herring, Polish cucumbers
in newspaper, and on the gas
   a bristly hen still boiling into soup:
most gentle sloven, how I honour now
   all your enormous, unfastidious welcome.

And when the string of two brown carrier bags
   bit into your short fat fingers
you only muttered, doesn't matter
   doesn't matter. I didn't understand
why you continued living with a man
   who could not forgive you, could not

forgive your worst offence:
   your happiness in little.
Even a string of shells would give you pleasure,
   but we did not bring gifts often;
and now it is too late to thank you for
   the warmth of your wide bosom, and the dimpled arms
waiting to hug my own bewildered children.

The Old Tailor

Yellow and bitter even
when we first met I remember:
    lenses, already thick and insectivorous,
turning upon me their
    suspicious glare.

Your legend was familiar to me:
the sourlipped snarls your
plucky wife smiled through,
    the harshest sneers for
anyone rash enough to take you on.

I wonder, now, how miserable you were,
    a clever child at school,
forced out to work. When did you first put on
    that brutal mask of blind
ferocity, to hide the lonely certainty of failure?

Remembering Jean Rhys

— Is that the new moon, that
    fine white line on the night, look,
through the hotel window? Then she covered up
    enormous eyes, to hide the dangerous sign.
And some cowardice made me lie.

Too much ill-luck had already happened,
    I suppose. Now, in her seventies, however late,
I wanted her to be having a fling and a treat
    unworried by some message from the skies
she might believe.

She listened for a moment like a child,
    smiling, and yet I saw
under the blue credulity of her gaze
    a writer's spirit,
and that was not deceived.

Wild Fruit

Yesterday, I found an over-ripe quince,
   wrinkled and yellow, on the tree
and the sweet flesh smelled of
   stored apples in a half-remembered room

from a childhood as far off as another country,
   where the light was golden as
weeds by an autumn waterside, and all
   that pungent garden entered the house

and breathed its warmth in fruit. And I
   held to the memory all afternoon, even though
the whole fen sky glared white,
   and the thin November air tasted of snow.

Park Parade, Cambridge

In memory of Elizabeth Bishop

Your thoughts in later years must, sometimes,
have visited this one-time lodging house,
the wood then chocolate brown, the plaster
veined, this bedroom floating over
spongy grass down to a shallow river.

As a mild ghost, then, look with me tonight
under this slant roof out to where
the great oak lies, its foliage disguised
with flakes of light. Above us, clouds
in these wide skies remain as still as sandbars.

Sleeplessly, together, we can listen
to the quiet song of water, hidden
at the lock, and wait up for the first
hiss of cycle tyres and whistling builders.
Fellow asthmatics, we won't even cough

because for once my lungs are clean,
and you no longer need to fight for breath.
And though it is by chance now I inherit
this room, I shall draw both tenderness and strength
from the friendly toughness of your spirit.

Hamburg

For Martin

You gave us all the riches of the city;
opera, pool-halls, all-night
Cafe Stern, cold Pils, and laughter;
the taste of coffee
with the first newspapers

and Isestrasse, over the canal,
street market stalls piled up
with edible truffles, beans
of black locust, poppy-seed buns,
and living fish.

We watched three carp swim there
in a glass tank; and knew
the bite of each grim
Asian jaw was meant to crush no more
than muddy weeds against a horny palate,

fierce yet vegetarian.
When the strongest fish leapt out
slap at our feet, it was your hand
that checked my squeamish terror.
My bold son,

learning to live without protection now
other than grace and beauty,
how I bless your spirit, as I
call up voice and face
to give me courage in this lonely place.

New Year

Blue velvet, white satin, bone horn: once again
We are summoned today to consider mistakes and failures
into the shabby synagogue on Thompson's Lane.
Shopkeepers, scholars, children and middle-aged strangers
are gathering to mumble the ancient prayers,

because this is Rosh Hashonah, the New Year,
we have all come in out of the Cambridge streets
to look around and recognize the faces
of friends we almost think of as relations
and lost relations who never lived anywhere near.

How are we Jewish, and what brings us together
in this most puritan of protestant centres?
Are the others talking to God, or do they remember
filial duties, or are they puzzled
themselves at the nature of being displaced?

I sit and think of the love between brothers,
my sons, who never took to festivals
happily seated round a family table;
I remember their laughter rising up to my bedroom,
late at night, playing music and cards together.

And as I look back on too many surprises
and face up to next year's uncertainties,
somehow I find it easier and easier
to pray. And this September, hope at least for
perfumes rising from a scrubby hedge
if not from flowering Birds of Paradise.

NEW SONGS FOR DIDO
AND AENEAS

I

The day opens, bland
and milky-blue. A woman
is looking out at a rain-washed garden.
In her thought a wooden flute and
spice trees, and the sun
flashing off the bracelet at her wrist.
She is no longer waiting for something to happen.

Her quiet face observes
the evidence of an order
older than Greece, in whose protection
the courtyard holds the trees, and
all her memories stir as gently
as leaves that flicker on the wall below her:

A stranger already knocks at the gate of the palace.

2

After Europe, Dido, all winter
the days rushed through me
as if I were dead, the
brown sea pouring into the cities
at night, the rain-smell of fish,

and when you ask for my story, how
we came to be blown along your
dock-streets, pocked and scuffed,
I see only my mother laced in silk,
myopic, her small feet picking over rubble.

How to make you imagine
our squares and streets, the glass
like falls of water, the gold-leaf
in the opera houses. There were
summer birds golden as weeds,

the scent of coffee and halva
rising from marble tables,
and on dark afternoons
the trams grinding on wet rails
round the corners of plaster palaces

such a babble of Empire
now extinguished, we can
never go home, Dido,
only ghosts remain
to know that we exist.

3

Some pain has burnt a desert in your head,
   which spills into the room,
sexless and stony-eyed, you rock
   over the landscape of your sandy dead.

I cannot soothe or reach into your dream
   or recognize the ghosts you name, or even
nurse your shaken body into calm.
   You wake, exhausted: to meet daylight in hell,

as the damned wake up with pennies
   of departure, and the ash
of all their lives have left undone
   lying like talcum on the tongue.

4

Unrepentant, treacherous, lecherous
  we loved beauty, in the tenderness
of violins, or the gentle voice of a girl,
  but we built over the stink of our dead,
our rivers ran yellow with the forgotten.
  Dido, the cruel cannot be blessed.

This endless sunshine, frangipani, gulls calling:
  How can you ease my pain or give me rest?
Ours was the generation that opened the gates
  to all the filthy creatures that had waited
for centuries to lay our cities waste.
  Your village kingdom cannot heal me now.
In any case, the cruel cannot be blessed.

Things come too late to save.
  On the last boat, we sang
old prayers, and some dreamed of quiet,
  but the sea took most of us. And
I am not prepared for white soot, cold ash,
  or the red sands of Australia. Forget me,
Dido. The cruel cannot be blessed.

5

Back from the seashore
    plangent, uncertain;
speaking of duties,
    but weaker, frightened.

The monster you found
    so gentle a beauty, is
no stranger here to us.
    You call her Venus;

but she is a mollusc
    goddess, pink in orifice,
prey clamped sweetly
    deep inside her ocean flesh.

What good mother would
    throw you to the ruthless seas?
Only the harshest
    and meanest of the deities.

You speak of yellow afternoons,
    dark skies, wet streets. And I who
once let the whole building of my own
    kingdom stop, to care for you,

offer my counsel; since
   it is in my gift
to curse or bless: be prudent, for
   you put us both in peril.

6

Last night, my sad Creusa, quietly
   crept into my dream. As if
dry leaves could speak, she whispered,
   but I could not catch her words,
Dido, and I was afraid

of what had wakened her.
   She was a loyal wife, in times
when nothing was forbidden
   no pleasure thought too gross:
and contrition as poor-spirited as cowardice.

Shall I spread that disease
   over the known world in a single colour?
Dido, I swear that Venus' weather in the cave
   the day our mouths first opened to each other,
and sweetness ran in our veins, was innocent.

Monsters and blood I dream of now,
   and a long voyage, lost,
although the wind has filled our sails.
   I must not falter in my mission,
Dido, at whatever cost.

7

Now in your leaving I admit old age.
How else? a clutch of whiteness at the heart
dry lips and icy wrists, a scream
that cuts my face into a wooden gape

At night   awake   alone   alert
to cries of meat-eating birds,
the whinge of gristle on bone, I sit
propped up on pillows, choking

on the catarrh of tears.
Sick   and yet stubborn
I, who was once your nurse,
hold back the power of my ancient curse.

8

Now we leave harbour, I no longer
fear the years' exile
nor what serenity I've lost:
I shall be no footnote now or gloss.
Empire is mine.

New heirs will rise to impose their will
on strange planets that all still
remain unknown, and thus fulfil
my deepest lust.

In this I trust.

9

The pyre of pine
   and ilex is prepared
and moonlit herbs
   isn't that the tale
of Dido's final stroke
   to wet Aeneas' eyes
as smoke?

European lies:
   I come of harsher blood
long ago, the venom of
   scorpions ceased to harm
and I've learnt from
   cactus and desert grass
what to do without.

I recognize in you that
   juniper tree, top-heavy
with branches, who may be
   will try to seed
again in parched earth
   and salt land;
but will not stand.

While my own root
   goes deep, into soil where
mysterious waters keep their
   sources cool, and though my leaves
dry out, and the wild sands blow,
   I shall live my time.

And when my bones lie
   between white stones at last
and fine white dust
   rises over all, no one who
survives among the dead
   will scorn my ghost.

THREE SONGS FROM
ITHACA

I

My man is lost.
And yet his wisdom sings in my
innermost source of blood,
my flesh recalls his love.
We were one earth.

I hold the pain,
as I wait every day
to question sailors at the port,
and so endure their sly reports
of his delay.

No more than water
once to his moods,
even now though he lies
on a foreign coast,
I am drawn and pure;

and on his return
I shall bless the sea
and forgive whoever holds him
far away from me.
If he only lives.

Yet I sit stubborn here
as the granite of his kingdom.
My house is at risk
and my son within,
and I shall not abandon it.

Ithaca, his home, where else
should he look to find me?
Every night as I am weaving and waiting,
I call up the powers of
a helpless woman

praying for happiness,
Odysseus, as you rush on, unlit,
into the inner and
the under darkness where
all our dreams meet.

3

Who brings a message over
the threshold of my dream? It is
Hermes, the twister, the pivoter, to remind me
of strangers, returning, who speak in the language
of timberwolves, feeding on human flesh, sorcerer's prey.
And I blench at his voice.

But I straighten awake.
Even if he is sick, huddled up,
with a grey face and seamed, my old love,
looking fierce or mad, my
Odysseus, bitter or black, I am his,
as I held back my own death for this:
so now I rejoice.

SONGS FOR EURYDICE:
A SEQUENCE

For Arnold

The dead are strong.
That winter as you wandered,
   the cold continued, still
the brightness cut
   my shape into the snow:
I would have let you go.

   Your mother blew
my dust into your lips
   a powder white as cocaine,
my name, runs to your nerves
   and now I move again in your song.
You will not let me go.

   The dead are strong.
Although in darkness I was lost
   and had forgotten all pain
long ago: in your song
   my lit face remains
and so we go

over pools that crack
like glass, through forests shining
   black with twigs that wait
for you to wake them, I return
   in your praise, as Eurydice's
ghost I light the trees.

   The dead are strong.

2

River, green river, forget
   your worm-eaten gods,
for we come to sweeten you,
   feel how the air has grown
warm and wet now
   the winds have all fallen.

On bent willow boughs
   beads of yellow break open
winter creatures we roused
   giant beeches and scrubland
in white roots respond
   Orpheus   Orpheus

We release all the woodlands
    from sleep, and the predator birds
from their hungering,
    wild cats are calm
as we pass

    as we reach the fields
men with grey knuckles
    lean over furrows
and blink.
    In the villages
wives honed too thin
    with their riverside washing
now straighten up,
    listen and nod.
What are they remembering?

    In cities, the traders
leave market stalls; even
    the rich leave their
food tureens. No one
    collects or cleans
their dirty crockery.

    Click! All transistors off.
Traffic stops. In
    a voice, everyone
hears how much
    any soul touched
by such magic is human

3

A path of cinders, I remember
   and limping upward
not yet uprooted from
   my dream, a ghost

with matted eyes, air–sacs
   rasping, white
brain, I staggered
   after you

Orpheus, when you first
   called, I pushed
the sweet earth from my mouth
   and sucked in

all the powders of volcanic ash
   to follow you
obedient up
   the crumbling slope

to the very last ridge –
   where I saw clumps of
yellow camomile in the dunes
   and heard the applause

of your wild mother
   great Calliope
crying good, my son, good
   in the fumes of the crater.

When the wiring sputtered
   at my wedding feast
she was hectic, glittering;
   her Arabian glass

burst into darkness
   and her flesh shimmered.
She was still laughing, there,
   on that pumice edge

with all Apollo's day behind her
   as I saw your heavy
shoulders turn. Your lips move.
   Then your eyes.

and I lay choking   Orpheus
   what hurt most then was
your stunned face
   lost

cruel   never to be touched
   again,   and watching
a blown leaf in your
   murderous eye

shrivel . . .

A storyteller cannot depict
even a tree without
    wind and weather: in your song

I was changed and reborn.
    when you asked for my innermost
thoughts, once, they lapped

    under shadows in shallows,
I never could find them:
    you wanted my soul,

water creature I was, all my life
    I had loved you in silence:
it was not what you wanted.

    My thoughts flew through pebbles
alight with the flash
    of my silvery sisters

in whispers between us.
    You wanted my soul,
though I shivered and bleached,

and it slipped from us both
when the snake bit my foot
    I was white as a moth.

In your song I am whole.

5

Over many centuries
modest ladies
who long for splendour
            gather here

their eyes most tender
their voices low
and their skins still clear
            when they appear

and to Dionysus
they offer their bodies
            for what they seek

The god of abandon
destroys their reason
            Beware the meek!

6

You belonged to Apollo
   the gold one   the cold one
and you were his servant:
   he could not protect you.

You called for your mother
   and her holy sisters
she wept as a witness:
   but could not protect you.

Here they come, murderers,
   their bodies spattered
with blood as they stagger
   off-balance towards you.

They claw and maul you
   with hoes and long mattocks
their heavy rakes tear at your
   throat and your fingers.

They batter the listening
   birds, and the oxen
at plough, and they share out
   the limbs of each creature they kill.

Any my love's head is thrown
    on the waters, it floats
singing still. All the
    nine Muses mourn,

Orpheus   Orpheus –
    for how many poets
must die at the hands
    of such revellers?

7

And the curse of all future
    poets to die by
rope or stake or fire falls there
    on these mindless creatures

no longer human their toes
    grow roots and their knees are
gnarled – their arms branch leaves:
    who will release them?

Their flesh is wood.

As dreamers now together
we forget Apollo's day
   that cruel light in which at last
all men become shadows;
   and we forgive even those
dead gods, who sleep among us.
   For all their gifts, not one
of them has power to summon us.
   In this green silence
we conceal our one true marriage.

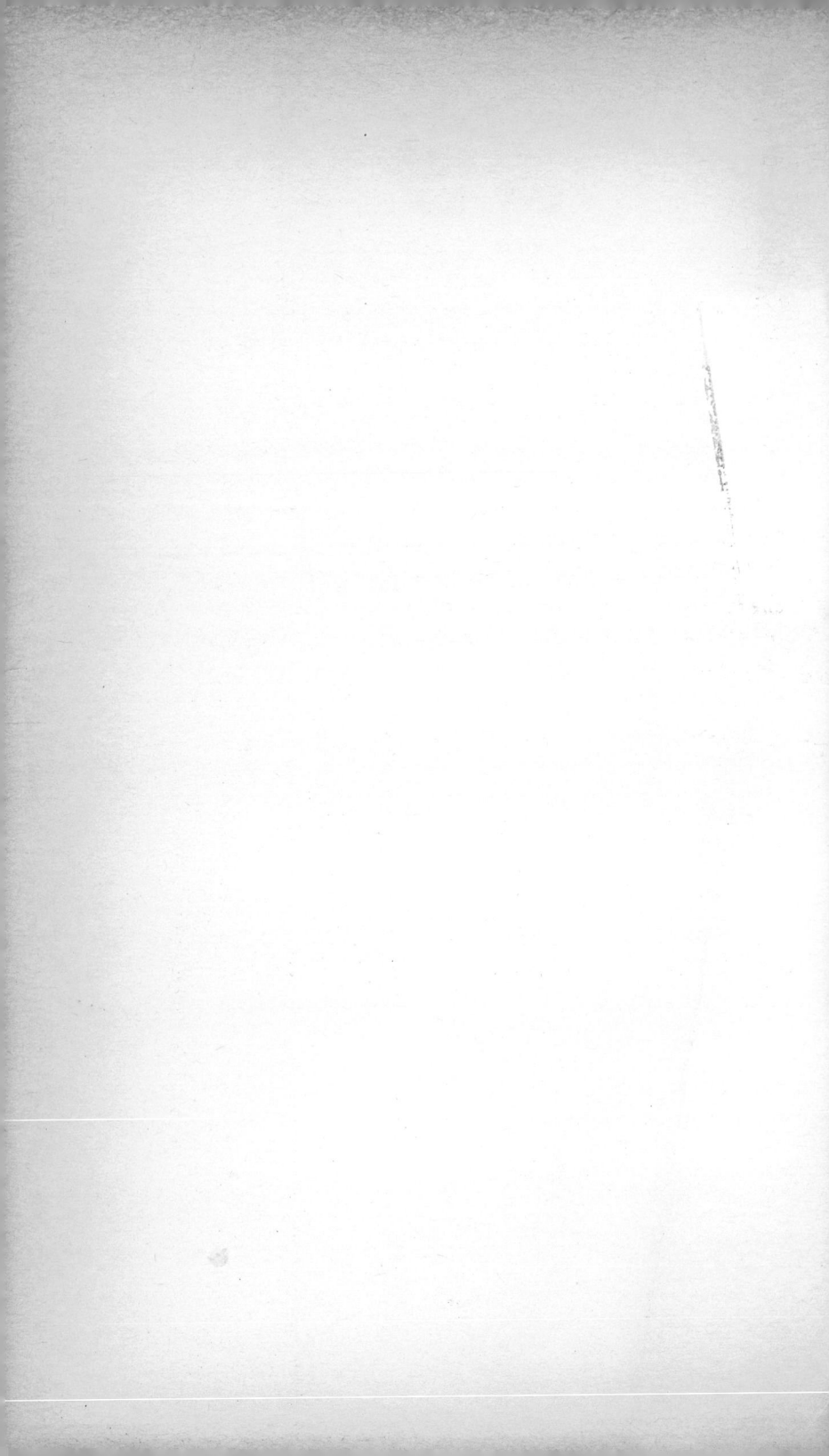